THIS BOOK BELONGS TO:

____

Write your name on the line above.

Illustrations by Lauren Greiner

Self-published by Lorena Espy

Broken Arrow, OK

ISBN: 979-8-234-07792-9 (Paperback)

Printed in the USA

First Edition

www.faithfuelsmyfire.com

You Are Loved

Color along with the story to
see how God's love for you
is so **BIG**!

WRITTEN BY LORENA ESPY
Illustrated by Lauren Greiner

In the beginning God made the HEAVENS and the EARTH.

God said, "LET THERE BE LIGHT," and He saw that the light was good. He separated the light from the darkness. God called the light "DAY" and the darkness "NIGHT."

God made the SKY, the SUN, the MOON, and the STARS.

God made the dry LAND and the SEAS.

Then God said, "Let the earth produce PLANTS and FRUIT TREES."

God made all of the animals like the LION, MONKEY, WOLF, MOUSE, SHEEP, and BIRDS.

Then God made His FAVORITE CREATION of all...

PEOPLE

(that's you and me)!

He made us because

HE LOVES US

and wants us to be a part of His FAMILY.

The first people that God made to be a part of His family were named "ADAM" and "EVE." God placed them in the garden of Eden to work it and watch over it. God told them that they could eat from any tree in the garden except for the tree of the KNOWLEDGE OF GOOD AND EVIL.

But we (and God) have a real ENEMY. His name is the DEVIL.

The devil came to Adam and Eve as a SERPENT to TRICK them. HE LIED to them and made them doubt what God said. THEY LISTENED to the devil and DISOBEYED God by eating the fruit from the tree of the knowledge of good and evil.

Because Adam and Eve disobeyed God, SIN entered the world, and we were SEPARATED from GOD. Now we all sin (do bad things) and need a

SAVIOR.

GOD LOVES US so much that He didn't want us to be separated from Him. He sent His **ONLY SON, JESUS,** to the earth to save us.

While Jesus lived on the earth, He was **WATER BAPTIZED** by His cousin John. The **HOLY SPIRIT** rested on Jesus like a dove (but the Holy Spirit isn't actually a bird).

Jesus lived a perfect life without sin (He never did anything bad.) God the Father was very pleased with Him.

With POWER from the Holy Spirit, Jesus TAUGHT and HEALED people. He opened the EYES of the BLIND so that they could SEE.

Some PEOPLE HATED Jesus and wanted to kill Him because they didn't believe that He was the SON OF GOD, so they hung Him on a

CROSS

to die. Jesus suffered a horrible DEATH for us (because He loves us so much). He willingly gave HIS LIFE for us.

JESVS
KING OF THE JEWS

But that's not the end of the story... 3 days later

JESUS ROSE FROM THE DEAD!

He defeated death and He is still ALIVE today! Jesus paid the price for our sins. He died for us so that we can have ETERNAL LIFE in Heaven with Him and God the Father. All we have to do is BELIEVE in Jesus, ask Him to come into our HEARTS, and FORGIVE us of our sins. Jesus is the only way to HEAVEN.

DO YOU BELIEVE what you have read about **JESUS** today? Jesus wants to **FORGIVE YOU** and give you **ETERNAL LIFE**. God wants to have a **PERSONAL RELATIONSHIP** with you and **NEVER** be separated from you again!

If you believe that **JESUS IS REAL** and that He is the only way into Heaven, say this prayer **OUT LOUD**:

If you said that prayer and meant it with **ALL YOUR HEART**, you are now a

Child of God

WELCOME TO THE FAMILY!

SO, WHAT NOW?

Now that you have become a child of God and have the HOLY SPIRIT within you, you can live a life free from sin and not do bad things. The Holy Spirit gives us the power to LIVE LIKE JESUS. You can now do the same things that Jesus did while He was on earth, such as HELPING, HEALING, LOVING, and SERVING OTHERS.

NEXT STEPS:

1. Let the Holy Spirit guide you

- Pray to God the Father and ask the Holy Spirit to guide you every day.
- The Holy Spirit will help you through life and show you things to come.

2. Get a Bible/read the Bible

- The Bible is full of God's words, and is His love story to us.
- If you've never read the Bible before, start in the book of John.

3. Go to church

- It's important to be around other people that love Jesus and want the best for you.
- God made us to be in relationship with Him and with others.

4. Get water baptized

- This is a way to show your commitment to follow Jesus.

5. Tell others about Jesus

- It's important for us to let others know about Jesus so that they may also be saved by Him.

ADDITIONAL QUESTIONS:

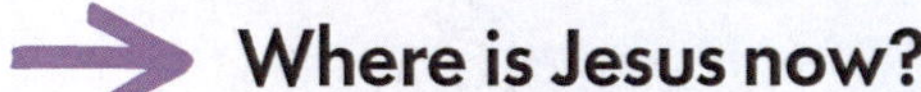

Where is Jesus now?

- In Heaven with God the Father, sitting at His right hand.

Who is the Holy Spirit?

- The Holy Spirit is our helper. He is God that lives inside of us once we are saved by Jesus. He guides us through life.

KEY SCRIPTURES FROM THE STORY:

1. **God's creation and sin entering the world:** Genesis 1-3
2. **God sent His Son Jesus:** John 3:16-17
3. **Jesus's baptism:** Matthew 3:13-17, Mark 1:9-11, Luke 3:21-22, John 1:29-34
4. **Jesus teaching people:** Matthew 4:23-25, Mark 1:14-15, Luke 4:14-15, John 13:13-17
5. **Jesus healing the blind:** John 9:1-39, Matthew 9:27-31, Mark 10:46-52, Mark 8:22-26
6. **Jesus dying on the cross:** Matthew 27, Mark 15, Luke 23, John 19
7. **Jesus rising from the dead:** Matthew 28:1-10, Mark 16:1-8, Luke 24, John 20:11-18

Try reading the Bible every day for 5 minutes.

Jesus LOVES you!

ABOUT THE AUTHOR

LORENA ESPY is a Christian author and podcast host of *Faith Fuels My Fire: The Podcast*. Originally from Bowling Green, Kentucky, she now lives in the Tulsa, Oklahoma area. She loves sharing God's Word and helping others grow in their faith. Her first published work was a 90-day devotional journal titled *Christ Transforms Me*.

Lorena wrote *You Are Loved: An Interactive Gospel Storybook for Children* with a heart to help children understand the simple gospel in a clear and meaningful way. Her desire is for kids to know how deeply God loves them, to be saved by Jesus, and to grow in their relationship with Him.

Learn more at FAITHFUELSMYFIRE.COM
Instagram: @LORENAESPY

ABOUT THE ILLUSTRATOR

LAUREN GREINER is a designer and illustrator based in Tulsa, Oklahoma. She creates vibrant illustrations that combine a whimsical style with realistic details. Her love of drawing started in childhood with Disney movies and Japanese anime. She received a BA in both Graphic Design and Painting from Anderson University in 2012. Lauren is currently pursuing her calling in missions work around the world. She hopes that her drawings inspire people of all ages to draw near to Jesus and learn about how much He loves them.

Instagram: @JOURNEY_WITH_LG

www.ingramcontent.com/pod-product-compliance
Ingram Content Group UK Ltd.
Pitfield, Milton Keynes, MK11 3LW, UK
UKRC030632300726
14130UKWH00011B/27

* 9 7 9 8 2 3 4 0 7 7 9 2 9 *

9 798234 077929